Greetings from
Abbotsbury

"*Legend*" Series No. 5. Published by R. R. Edwards, 4, Castle Street, Salisbury, Wiltshire, England.

A DORSETSHIRE LEGEND.

In an old Church dedicated to St. Catherine, there is a hole in the inside wall, east of the South door, into which, it is said, ladies put one of their hands, stretching the other out on the wall, saying :

"St. Catherine I pray thee lend me thy aid,
Let me not, let me not, die an old maid."

(The Church of St. Catherine is situated at Abbotsbury).

A Dorsetshire Legend. Unused, pre-1914. Published by R. Edwards, Salisbury, from a drawing by Edith Ewen. References to the apparently potent power of St Catherine, or St Catharine as it is often spelt, are common in Abbotsbury guide books and postcards from the late Victorian period. The hole in the chapel wall is still there, but perhaps the fear of spinsterhood is not as great today as it was when this card was published.

Greetings from
Abbotsbury

THE STORY OF A DORSET VILLAGE
IN POSTCARDS

Paul Atterbury

With postcards from the collection of
David Stevens

POST CARD
PRESS

ACKNOWLEDGEMENTS

We should like to thank David Stevens and Peter Cove for their help in compiling this book and the use of their postcards. Without their enthusiasm for all things Abbotsbury and their passion for postcards this book would not have been possible.
David Stevens would like to thank his wife Heather, for putting up with him and all things Abbotsbury for thirty years, and his mother, Emily Stevens, for her invaluable contribution.
Wherever possible, publishers and photographers of postcards have beed credited in the captions. We have used our best endeavours to trace the copyright holders of postcard images issued by photographers or publishers no longer in business.
In the production of this book, a number of other books have been invaluable. These include:
T. Cooper, *Pictorial Guide to Abbotsbury*, published by the author, 1895.
John Fair, Don Moxom and Petyo Slatter, *Abbotsbury and the Swannery*, Dovecote Press, Wimborne, 1993.
Trustees of the Strangways Estate, *An Appreciation of Abbotsbury*, 1973.

Arms of Sir John Strangways on the
ceiling of the Parish Church.

Front cover: Detail from The Barn at Abbotsbury, an Oilette card in the Picturesque Dorset series.
Back cover: Swans and Cygnets, The Swannery, Abbotsbury.

Text copyright Paul Atterbury. All rights reserved. A CIP catalogue record for this book is available from the British Library.

First published in Great Britain in 2004 by the Postcard Press, Whin Bridge, Eype, Bridport, Dorset DT6 6AL
Printed and bound in Great Britain by Creeds, Broadoak, Bridport, Dorset DT6 5NL

ISBN 0-9545372-1-1

The publishers will be delighted to hear about postcard images of Abbotsbury not included in this book, or about any photographs, documents, records or personal memories relevant to the history of Abbotsbury and its inhabitants.

USING THE BOOK

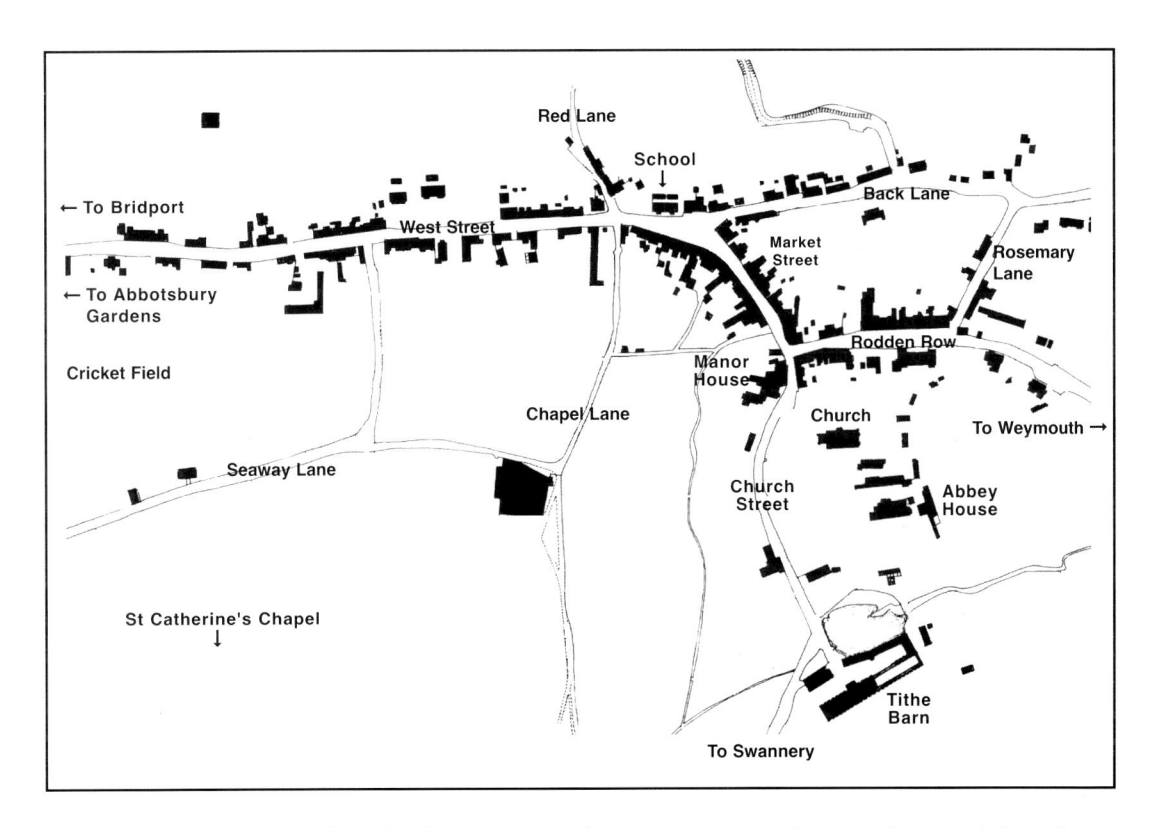

The postcards illustrated in this book start with general views of Abbotsbury and then focus on the main buildings. Next come views of the streets arranged geographically, starting at the western end. A large section then follows, devoted to village life. The final selection of cards document the gardens and the swannery. Throughout, cards are presented in chronological, or date order. When relevant the viewpoint of the card is identified so that anyone wanting to explore the village and find the locations can do so. Most are easily accessible, and in many cases little has changed. The outline map above shows the plan of the village and its key streets and buildings.

Postmark dates on the cards are given when known, even though these are only helpful up to a point. Many postcards remained in use for long periods, and the photographs used were, in many cases, taken long before the postmark date. When estimated dates are given, they are based on internal evidence in the card and on comparisons with other cards by the same publisher. Many of the cards included in this book are unused, indicating that postcard collecting was a flourishing activity, particularly in the period before the First World War. Clearly, many were purchased as souvenirs, and so there are many versions of the more popular views. Others of a more personal nature were photographs printed onto postcard-backed photographic paper, a common phenomenon of the Edwardian era and the 1920s and 1930s. Such cards were made in very small numbers and may in some cases be unique.

The Temperance movement was very strong in Victorian Britain, particularly in remote rural areas where the influence of the church was still powerful. This abstention declaration, or pledge, was issued in Abbotsbury in March 1896 to Leonora White.

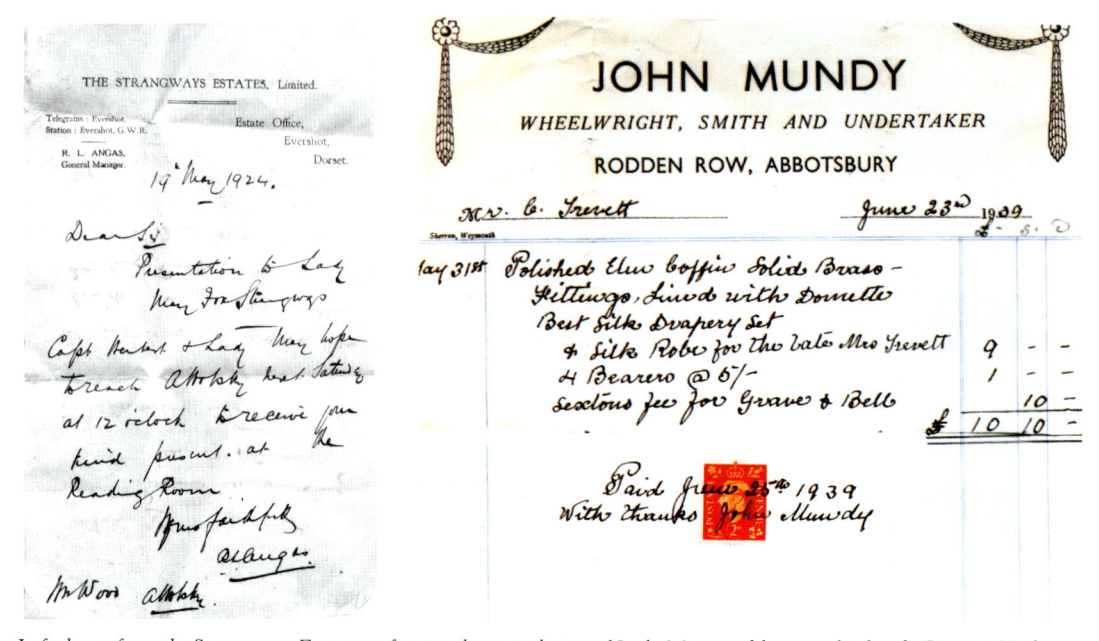

Left: letter from the Strangways Estate confirming the arrival time of Lady Mary and her new husband, Captain Herbert, to receive their wedding presents from the villagers of Abbotsbury in May 1924 (see page 62). Right: Invoice from John Mundy, wheelwright and undertaker of Rodden Row for the funeral arrangements for Mrs Trevett in June 1939.

THE STORY OF ABBOTSBURY

As befits a village of such distinct character and so splendid a setting, Abbotsbury has been settled at least since the Bronze Age, as revealed by the seventeen burial barrows on the ridge above the village. In the Iron Age a hillfort whose double ramparts enclose four acres was built to the north west of the village. In use possibly until the Roman occupation, and still visible today, this hillfort is known as Abbotsbury Castle. Little is known about the period of Roman occupation and the centuries that followed. Not until the tenth century does the name of Abbotsbury first appear, in a land grant. Although the name means the abbot's town, it seems to have emerged before the monastery was founded.

The history of the village really starts in 1023 when the Viking Orc, steward to King Canute, was granted land at Abbotsbury by Canute, a grant that can still be seen in Dorset's oldest document. Orc and his wife Tola acquired the land with the aim of founding a monastery, something that took place in about 1040. After Canute's death, Orc became steward to Edward the Confessor, and it was Edward who gave him the sea shore bordering his lands and rights to all wrecks. When Orc died, he was buried in the monastery he had founded. In the seventeenth century the historian Thomas Gerard reported seeing Orc's bones in a stone coffin, but they were subsequently lost

The Benedictine monastery founded by Orc became large and powerful and by the Middle Ages it was one of the wealthiest in Dorset, owning 2,000 acres in the parish, and other lands and building around West Dorset. It included two churches, St Peter for the use of the monks, and St Nicholas for the village. St Peter's has completely vanished but it was by all accounts a massive building over 250 feet long, complete with cloisters and a large central tower. Self-sufficient as always, the monastery had its own mill, dovecot and fishponds, as well as the great tithe barn. The monks also benefitted from the nearby swannery, probably in existence well before 1393, when it is first documented.

Little is known about the history of the monastery, other than that it was famous for its scriptorium and library, which housed many illuminated manuscripts produced here and elsewhere. Stories and legends surround the lives of some of the abbots. One kept hunting dogs, had too many servants and refused to eat with the other monks, while another died from the Black Death. Particularly infamous was the last abbot, Roger Hardie, accused of stealing plate and jewels and keeping a large harem in the monastic buildings. In 1539 Abbotsbury monastery was dissolved on the orders of Henry VIII. At that point there were nine monks and the annual income was £400. Following the dissolution, Hardie survived to become vicar of Abbotsbury, but most of the monastery was eventually destroyed. As in so many similar cases all over England, the monastic buildings were used as a convenient source of stone, and fragments can be identified in a number of Abbotsbury houses. Two major structures survived, the tithe barn and St Catherine's chapel, although the former was greatly reduced in size. St Catherine's chapel, set high on a hill overlooking the village and the sea and surrounded by the remains of medieval fields cut into the hillside, was already established as a navigational mark for sailors in Lyme Bay. For this reason it was left intact. It would be tempting to think that it was also spared because of the succour it offered to spinsters, who on one day in the year could pray for a husband from their patron saint, St Catherine. This ancient legend is perennially popular, and many versions of the spinster's prayer have been recorded, including this typically Dorset example:

> Sweet St Catherine send me a husband.
> A good one I pray.
> But arn-a-one better than narn-a-one
> Oh St Catherine, lend me thine aid,
> And grant that I never may die an old maid.

In 1543 Sir Giles Strangways, one of the commissioners appointed by Henry VIII to oversee the surrender of monasteries, monastic lands and possessions, bought the abbey and all its buildings and lands, including the swannery. The Strangways were a Yorkshire family who had moved south at the end of the fifteenth century and settled near Dorchester. Sir Giles's father Thomas was buried at the abbey in 1505 and the family had founded a chantry there, events that may have influenced the purchase. This was the beginning of an association between Abbotsbury and the Strangways family that has lasted over 450 years and spanned fifteen generations. Having supervised the destruction of the monastic buildings, Sir Giles used some of the stone to erect a substantial house on the site of the abbey.

A thriving market town and a centre of local trade during the life of the monastery, Abbotsbury now entered a period of decline. The weekly market ceased and the inhabitants that remained earned a basic living on the land or from fishing. In 1635 the historian Coker wrote: 'Abbotsbury towne is but poore, the chiefest trade consists in fishing.' The situation was not improved by the outbreak of the Civil War in 1640, for Sir John Strangways was a staunch Royalist. In 1643 his house was ransacked by Parliamentary troops and then, in November 1644, a large Parliamentary force under the command of Sir Anthony Ashley Cooper was sent from Dorchester to stamp out the Royalist garrison in the village. A fierce battle followed, lasting over six hours, before the garrison was defeated. The house was completely destroyed by fire and a powder explosion, and Sir John Strangways and his son Giles were later captured and sent to the Tower of London for three years and fined the massive sum of £10,000. Sir John's other son James, the colonel of the Royalist garrison, escaped to France.

The restoration of Charles II brought stability and status back to the Strangways, but for Abbotsbury it was a different story as the village experienced decades of poverty and misfortune. In 1706 much of the western half of the village was destroyed by fire, hindering further the lives of the villagers who gained a meagre existence from farming, fishing and cotton spinning. It was this continual hardship, combined with the convenient isolation of Chesil Bank, that turned Abbotsbury into a centre for smuggling. In 1752 a writer in the London Journal claimed that 'All the people of Abbotsbury, including the Vicar, are thieves, smugglers and plunderers of wrecks.' In the eighteenth century, smuggling was a highly organised activity with gangs operating regularly along the Dorset coast and bringing large quantities of tea, wine, brandy, tobacco and other commodities into the country, despite the efforts of the revenue and customs officers. With a duty of four shillings per pound, tea was particularly popular with the smugglers and in 1743 it was calculated that two-thirds of the tea brought into Britain was contraband. There are a number of records of confrontations on Chesil. In September 1743, for example, a boatload of smugglers was chased ashore near Abbotsbury and captured by the local customs officer who, to his amazement, took possession of over 900 pounds of tobacco, 200 pounds of tea and large quantities of brandy and rum. In 1815 Benjamin Brown, the local customs officer, reported that 'the mode of smuggling carried on is by means of sinking small casks of spirits in the Fleet, and getting them up as opportunity offers.' By the 1840s, this kind of local smuggling had come to an end, but even then ten men and one woman from Abbotsbury were convicted of smuggling between 1817 and 1843.

In other ways, the fortunes of Abbotsbury began to revive from the middle of the eighteenth century, notably after the marriage of Elizabeth Strangways Horner to Stephen Fox, later the 1st Earl of Ilchester. In 1765 she built the first Abbotsbury Castle, and established the famous gardens. A few years earlier Abbotsbury's first school had opened, funded by Elizabeth's mother. In 1776 toll roads greatly improved the village's connections with Bridport and Weymouth. New industries, including basket and rope-making, were established, and the population rose steadily, reaching its peak of 1,089 in 1861. A new school was opened in 1858, funded by the Earl of Ilchester, along with many of the cottages that are still to be seen in the village. In 1880, as well as farm workers and fishermen, Abbotsbury

Ford's provisions shop in Market Street in the late Victorian era, with Mr Ford in the foreground and his daughter in the doorway.

supported blacksmiths, bakers, bootmakers, wheelwrights, carpenters, thatchers, tailors and grocers, as well as a saddler, a cooper and a miller, an indication that it was a thriving community. Another important local industry has been the management of the reed beds, traditionally the source of the thatch used on so many of the local houses Unlike the other local crafts and professions listed above, this still survives today, supplying reeds for thatching and for bedding for the swans. A century ago the reed beds also supplied large quantities of willow, used for fencing posts and hurdles, for staples for pinning the thatch, for basket making and for bundles of faggots for the baker's oven.

Tourism was also an important new industry and the first Abbotsbury guide book was written and published in 1895 by T. Cooper, the proprietor of the Ilchester Arms family hotel, described at the time as 'replete with every comfort for visitors.' By then, the railway had arrived, a branch line from Upwey on the Weymouth to Bristol line having been opened in 1885. Local deposits of iron ore, then thought to be measured in millions of tons and easily accessed from open quarries, were the primary inspiration for the building of the line, whose route came via Portesham. In the event, the iron ore trade never got going, and so the Abbotsbury railway had to survive from tourism and the transport of local necessities, which it continued to do until 1952.

Abbotsbury had a number of attractions that appealed to visitors, including the tithe barn, St Catherine's chapel and Chesil beach, as well as the picturesque quality of the village itself and its setting. There is plenty of evidence of family and social groups making day trips to the village from Weymouth and other large towns in the late Victorian and Edwardian eras, and they would certainly have come by train. After the First World War motor buses and private cars began to compete with the railway and so the popularity of Abbotsbury gradually spread, even though the village's population was in steady decline. However, the main attractions were always the gardens and the swannery.

In 1765 Elizabeth, 1st Countess of Ilchester, built a castle-like summer residence high on a hillside overlooking Lyme Bay, to the west of the village. This, the first Abbotsbury Castle, remained in use until 1913, when it was destroyed by fire. Subsequently rebuilt, it was abandoned and demolished in 1934. The countess also laid out a garden in a valley below the castle, and this was the foundation for the famous sub-tropical gardens which have flourished for over 250 years, thanks to the combination of a warm and sheltered setting and sandy soil. Subsequent generations of the family have expanded and developed the garden, which now includes rare and exotic plants and trees from China, Japan, India and the Himalayas, Australia and New Zealand, Mexico and South America and all around the Mediterranean. Some are directly descended from late eighteenth-century introductions, notably camellias from Japan in 1792 and olive trees from Madeira in 1784. Woodlands were added early in the nineteenth century and later the lily ponds were developed. At the same time, walks were planned and laid out, in response to the large increase in the number of visitors after the opening of the railway. A catalogue of the garden issued in 1899 lists over 5,000 species, while Mr Cooper's guide book mentions camellias, azaleas, eucalyptus, fan palms, cork trees, figs, cacti, rhododendrons, bamboos, tea trees, strawberry trees, wattle, quince and, as he says 'others too numerous to quote.'

The first recorded mention of the swannery is in a monk's court roll of 1393, but it was certainly in existence long before then and may have been there when the monastery was

Primitive carving of the Trinity, dating from the Saxon period, set into the tower above the west door of the church.

CATTISTOCK HOUNDS.

MASTER—

Reginald Chandos Pole, Esq.

MEETS NEAR ABBOTSBURY

Look. Berwick. Traveller's Rest. Loaders. Askerswell. Kingston Russell. Winterborne Steepleton, Martin's-town. Monument. Ridgeway Hill. Upwey. Buckland Ripers. Corfe Hill. Fleet. Portisham.

"ILCHESTER ARMS" Family Hotel, ABBOTSBURY, DORSET.

Patronised by T.R.H. Duke and Duchess of Edinburgh.
  " H.R.H. Duke of Connaught.
  " H.S.H. Prince Edward of Saxe Weimar.

This old-established Family Hotel having recently been considerably improved, is now replete with every comfort and accommodation for Visitors. The Hotel is in close proximity with, and commands views of the far famed West Bay and Chesil Beach, St. Catherine's Chapel, the Abbey Ruins, the Earl of Ilchester's splendid Swannery and Semi-Tropical Gardens, all within a short distance of the Hotel.

A Public Dining Room, Drawing Room, Private Sitting Rooms; cleanly, quiet, and home comforts, with personal attention.

Good Stabling & Lock=up Coach House.
BILLIARDS.
—TARIFF ON APPLICATION.—

T. COOPER, *Proprietor.*

Advertisements from T. Cooper's Pictorial Guide to Abbotsbury, 1895.

established in the eleventh century. The swans provided the monks with eggs and meat, down for pillows and quills for writing, and so the swannery was a vital source of both sustinence and income. All swans on open water belong to the monarch, the only exceptions being those on the River Thames, owned by the Worshipful Company of Vintners and Dyers, and the Abbotsbury herd, owned until the dissolution by the abbey, and subsequently by the Strangways family. All birds in the herd are marked and ringed, a process of identification that has gone on since the Middle Ages, but they are always free to come and go at will. For the swans, the main attraction is the Fleet, which offers both shelter and an abundant supply of food. The only time the herd is managed is at breeding time, and this management is under the control of the swanherd, a post that has probably existed since the founding of the abbey. The sight of the swans, particularly at breeding time when the cygnets appear, has been popular with visitors for centuries, but the tourist potential of the swannery has mainly been developed since the late Victorian period. Since then, the breeding season and the round-up during the moult in July, when hundreds of swans are captured for marking and ringing, have attracted increasing numbers of visitors. In winter, the sight of many thousands of waterfowl on the Fleet is also memorable.

Adjacent to the swannery is the duck decoy. This was constructed by Sir John Strangways in about 1655 and today it is the oldest and the most original still in use in Britain. The decoy is in the form of a netted and curved tunnel, sealed at the far end, into which duck and other wildfowl are lured. Such decoys were once commonplace as sources of food, but now only five are known in Britain. Since the 1930s, ducks caught in the decoy have increasingly been ringed and released.

The popularity of Abbotsbury in the twentieth century is reflected by the number of postcards issued by many photographers and publishers since the early 1900s. Many hundreds have been recorded by collectors. Most show variations on popular and well known views, but there are many that are more individual, offering an insight into the history of Abbotsbury and its inhabitants. All parts of the village are covered. The earliest card in the book dates from about 1904 and the latest from the 1960s. The majority were issued by publishers in Weymouth, but others came from Bridport, Evershot and Bristol. As with so many cards of this period, a large number are anonymous. Today, Abbotsbury is more popular than ever and its picturesque streets are lined with cafes and restaurants, souvenir shops and art and craft galleries. The appeal of the village today is its unchanging nature, a particular quality brought to life by the century of postcards included in this book.

Abbotsbury Village. Postmark 8th September 1910. Published by Welch & Sons, Portsmouth and printed in Belgium. This card shows the classic view of Abbotsbury from the north west, with the heart of the village around the church, a view that is little changed today.

Abbotsbury. Postmark 24th December 1904. No publisher. A view from the south east with the Abbey barn in the foreground. Overprinted to be used as a Christmas card, and posted on the afternoon of Christmas Eve in Weymouth with the certainty that it would be delivered to Bridport in time for Christmas.

St Nicholas Church, Abbotsbury. Unused, pre-1914. No publisher. The church, seen from the north east, looks in very good order in this card, no doubt the result of the very thorough restoration of 1886. This view shows well the massive nature of the tower and the series of round-headed seventeenth century windows.

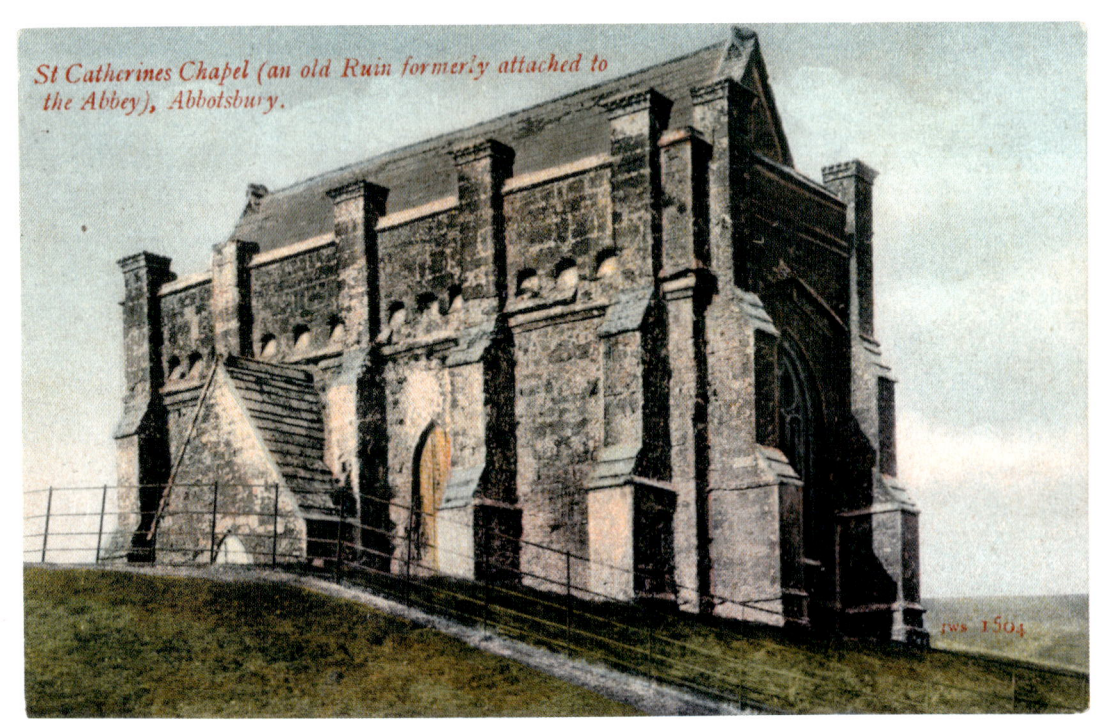

St Catherine's Chapel (an old ruin formerly attached to the Abbey), Abbotsbury. Unused, pre-1914. Published by Welch & Sons, Portsmouth and printed in Belgium. The sturdy nature of the fourteenth-century chapel is apparent in this view which shows the great buttresses, built both to support the roof and to protect the building from the gales.

Picturesque Dorset. The Barn at Abbotsbury. Unused, pre-1918. Published by Tuck & Sons, in the Oilette series. This romantic view gives the barn, described as "one of the objects of interest testifying to Abbotsbury's antiquity... with decoration of an ecclesiastical nature', a delightfully rustic look. Images emphasising the picturesque nature of the countryside were popular at this time.

Old Abbey Gateway, Abbotsbury. Unused, pre-1914. Published by Welch & Sons and printed in Belgium. The so-called Abbey Gateway, a much photographed feature, was actually part of The Manor House built by Sir Giles Strangways and destroyed during the Civil War. On the hilltop is St Catherine's Chapel.

Ilchester Hotel, Abbotsbury. Postmark 12th October, 1932. Published by L. Wickwar, Post Office, Abbotsbury. A quiet day in the market place, the heart of the village. This is borne out by the message: 'This place has old memories it is quiet now & still very pretty.'

Rodden Row, Abbotsbury. Unused. Published by Tuck & Sons. This familiar view along one of Abbotsbury's most picturesque streets shows the raised pavement and the many thatched roofs, along with a pleasant lack of traffic. The ramp on the right leads to the workshop of Mr Mundy, wheelwright and coffin maker.

Abbotsbury, Castle & Chesil Beach. Postmark unclear but probably 1912. Published by Tuck & Sons for J. F. Gibbons, Post Office, Abbotsbury. Seen from the east, the castle is shown here before the fire of 1913 and its subsequent rebuilding. This early view is before the new coastguard cottages were built and before the new approach road.

The Beach, Abbotsbury. Unused, pre-1914. No publisher. Abbotsbury has traditionally regarded the adjacent section of Chesil Beach as a feature that turned it into a seaside village. In the past the haunt of wreckers and fishermen, it became in the Edwardian era popular with visitors, many of whom came by train.

Swans and Cygnets, The Swannery, Abbotsbury. Unused, pre-1920. Published by E. H. Seward, Weymouth. The Swannery has long been Abbotsbury's most popular attraction, with the appeal of the nesting birds and their young made clear by this artistic card.

A Corner of Abbotsbury Gardens (title on verso). Unused, probably 1950s. Published by W. Chudleigh & Son, Exeter.

Abbotsbury Multiview card, showing West Street, Trinity Carving on St Nicholas's Church, Interior of Church and Sunnyside. Unused, pre-1920. No publisher. This early multiview card is unusual in not including the major sights of Abbotsbury, such as the barn and St Catherine's chapel.

Greetings from Abbotsbury. Unused, 1920s. No publisher. A decorative multiview card with typical images.

Greetings from Abbotsbury. Unused, 1950s. No publisher. A multiview card with a typical series of images, all based on individual cards.

Abbotsbury, Dorset. Unused, probably 1940s. Published by Aero Pictorial Ltd. In this very clear aerial view from the north east most of Abbotsbury's key features can be identified, along with the road layout. The scene is remarkably empty of vehicles and people.

Abbotsbury. Unused, 1920s. Published by Seward, Weymouth, the Melcombe Series. This broad view from the north west places Abbotsbury in the context of its landscape, framed by hills and farmland, and backed by the Fleet and the sea.

Abbotsbury. Unused, 1920s. No publisher. A view from the south west, probably from St Catherine's Chapel, with West Street the focus.

Dorset Landscape, Abbotsbury. Unused, 1950s. No publisher. A view from the new barn road, leading to the swannery, with St Catherine's Chapel on the distant skyline. A notably empty landscape view which does not actually show the village at all.

Abbotsbury Village. Unused, pre-1918. Published by J. F. Gibbons, Post Office, Abbotsbury. A view from the north, showing the heart of the village. This popular image was issued by several publishers, in colour and monochrome versions.

Abbotsbury Showing Abbey Gateway. Unused, 1920s. No publisher. A similar view from the south. Despite the title, the Abbey gateway is quite hard to see, in the trees to the left. Much clearer is the tennis court in the foreground.

23

Abbotsbury. Postmark 8 August 1937. No publisher. A clear view from the south, with the ruined part of the barn in the foreground, and the village beyond. The sender, writing to friends in Chester, was staying in the Abbey House on the right. He says:'This is the most delightful place I have ever seen.'

Abbotsbury. Unused, pre-1918. Published by J. B. Green, Evershot. A view from the north west, looking towards Market Street and the Ilchester Arms. A feature of many of these general view cards are the remarkably tidy gardens and vegetable plots, as in the foreground here, beyond the chicken run.

Old Abbey Gateway, Abbotsbury. Unused, 1920s. Published by Seward, Weymouth. A familiar and much repeated view of the gateway framing St Catherine's Chapel. The people staying in the Abbey House (see card, top left) described entering through the gateway.

THE OLD MILL AND ST. CATHERINE'S CHAPEL, ABBOTSBURY

The Old Mill and St Catherine's Chapel. Unused, 1950s. No publisher. Set in the valley outside the village, the stone-built mill building seems rather derelict in this view. It was working in the 1900s and in the 1901 census three millers are listed in Abbotsbury. Out of use by the early 1920s, it has since been restored and converted into a house.

St Catherine's Chapel, Abbotsbury. Unused, 1920s. Published by Seward, Weymouth. An atmospheric view of the chapel, as seen from the path up from the village.

Abbey Gateway & Church, Abbotsbury. Unused, pre-1914. Photograph by H. Cumming. An unusual and carefully composed view, featuring contrasting types of stonework. The church tower is actually some distance away from the gateway, so the composition is a bit misleading.

Abbey Gateway, Abbotsbury. Unused, pre-1914. Published by Walter Cox, Weymouth. This delightful and well-constructed image is made much more appealing by the poses of the three little girls, an approach much favoured by late Victorian and Edwardian photographers.

Abbotsbury Church, Dorset. Unused, 1920s. Published by Seward, Weymouth. The sturdy west tower of the church is a straightforward fifteenth-century structure. The rather primitive carving of the Trinity can be seen inset above the window.

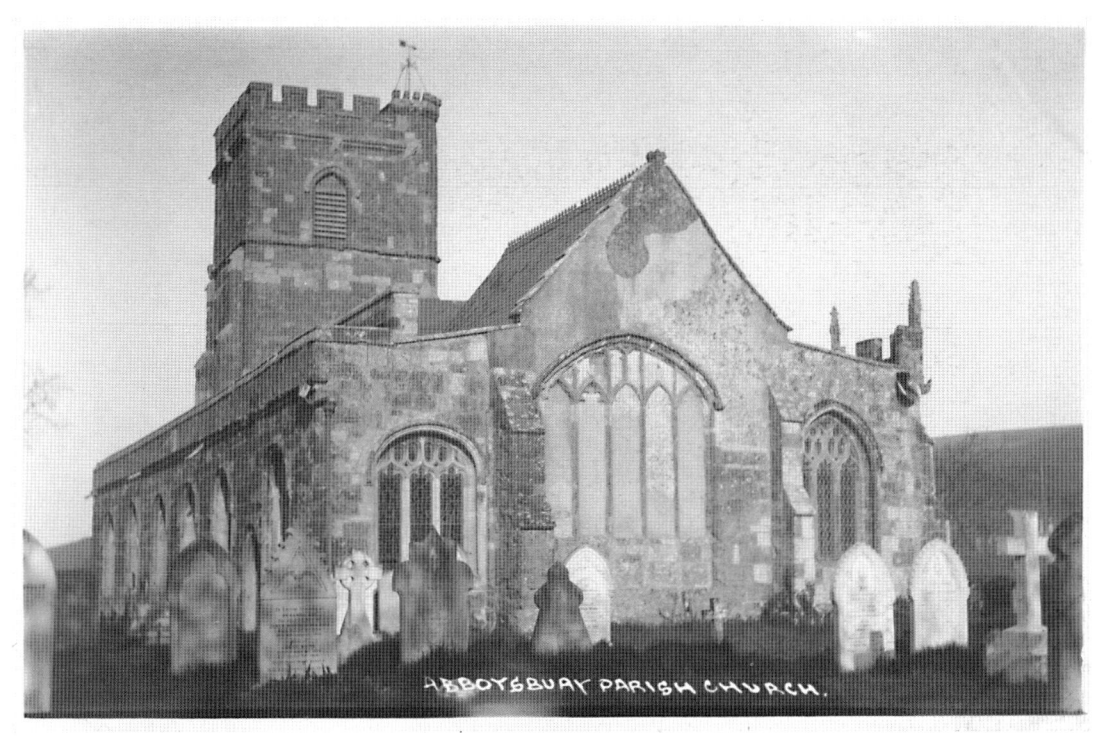

Abbotsbury Parish Church. Unused, 1920s. Published by Seward, Weymouth. From the east, the balanced and well-proportioned style of the church is apparent. The round-arched windows are probably seventeenth century.

Abbotsbury Ch. Dorset. Postmark 30th July 1908. Published by E. H. Seward, Weymouth. This interior view of the church shows well the classical reredos of 1751, the Jacobean pulpit and the pews which date from the 1886 restoration.

Stone Coffin, Abbotsbury. Unposted, but dated in pencil 31th August 1928. Published by Seward, Weymouth. One of the familiar sites of Abbotsbury is the group of medieval stone coffins, shown here and in the card below, incorporated into the churchyard wall.

Old Stone Coffins. Abbotsbury. Unused, 1920s. Published by Seward, Weymouth.

Untitled. Postmark 19th August 1921. No publisher. Judging by the crispness of the carving and the date of the postmark, this shows the war memorial shortly after it was erected. Thirteen names, listed here alphabetically without indication of service, rank or date of death, represent a significant loss for a village the size of Abbotsbury. By contrast, no one from the village was killed in action during the Second World War. The card, sent by Ivy to her mother in Dorchester, is rather out of step with the message: 'Having jolly time at Abbotsbury.'

Untitled. Postmark 19th March 1906. Published by J. B. Green, Evershot. This shows the Congregational Church built during the late Victorian era. It is now an artist's studio. The message reveals the great enthusiasm for postcard collecting at this time: 'We received some very fine P.C.s from Switzerland which we shall prize very highly.'

Tithe Barn Doorway, Abbotsbury. Unused, 1920s. Published by C. & S. Kestin, Weymouth. The barn is probably Abbotsbury's best known feature and can, as a result, be seen in many cards. The building is remarkable and, when built in the fourteenth century, was, at over 270 feet, one of the largest in England. What stands today is about half.

The Abbots Barn, Abbotsbury, Dorset. Postmark 1st September 1955. Published by Seward, Weymouth in the 1920s and reissued much later. The eleventh century barn is the most significant surviving part of the Benedictine monastery. The Abbey Church, which stood to the south of the present church, was a massive structure, with a nave 54 feet across. It is not clear what the group of people on the right are up to as the steep slope would be an uncomfortable picnic spot.

Tithe Barn, Abbotsbury. Unused, 1930s. No publisher. This view of the western gable end shows the powerful structure of the barn, with its great buttresses.

The Abbey Barn, Abbotsbury. unused, pre-1918. No publisher. This view shows the back of the barn. With so many cards produced over a wide time span, it is possible to see the changing state of repair at different times. The thatch is either tidy or in tatters, the stonework well repaired or crumbling. In this card, earlier than the one above, the same gable end is completely obscured by rampant climbers.

Abbotsbury Castle. Unused, pre-1913. Published by Seward, Weymouth. The real Abbotsbury Castle is an Iron Age hill fort covering ten acres, set high on a hill to the north west of the village. This Abbotsbury Castle was built in 1765 as a summer home for Elizabeth Strangways Horner, first Countess of Ilchester, with a wonderful view out across the bay. This card shows the rather random nature of the house, with evidence of later additions and rebuilding.

Abbotsbury Castle. Unused, pre-1913. Published by J. B. Green, Evershot.

Abbotsbury Castle Destroyed by Fire Febry 7th 1913. Unused. Published by Austin & Potts, Bridport. This card shows the complete devastation caused by the fire.

The Castle Abbotsbury. Postmark 1919, remainder illegible. Published by Seward, Weymouth. Following the fire, the castle was completely rebuilt in a more unified style. This photograph, taken soon after the rebuilding in 1915, shows all the rubble from the earlier castle dumped onto the hillside. The new castle did not last long, being completely demolished in 1934, partly as a result of poor quality materials used during the rebuilding.

Manor House Abbotsbury. Postmark 1904, remainder illegible. Photograph by H. Cumming. The Manor House, or Abbey House, is a haphazard mixture of sixteenth- and seventeenth-century structures, including some components of the original Abbey. This early view shows the picturesque nature of the house and its fine gardens.

Abbotsbury. Unused, pre-1914. Published by Seward, Weymouth. This shows The Manor from the road, at a slightly later date.

37

The Basket Maker. Unused, 1920s. Published by Seward, Weymouth. This card depicts Mr Dunford, the local thatcher, engaged in one of the traditional cottage industries of Abbotsbury. Seated outside a little thatched building still known as the Spar House, he made baskets in his spare time. By the 1920s crafts such as this were largely supported by tourism.

Thatch Cottage, Abbotsbury. Unused, 1920s. Published by Seward, Weymouth. A typically picturesque view of a cottage in Back Street, chosen at the time to capture the atmosphere of the village. It was occupied at the time by another member of the Dunford family, who sold coal from his outhouses, and delivered it around the village with a horse and cart. The coal was brought to Abbotsbury by train.

Abbotsbury. Unused, 1920s. Published by Seward, Weymouth. The approach to the village towards West Street in much quieter times. A number of accidents on this bend caused the road to be widened, probably by the early 1930s.

Abbotsbury Dorset. Unused, pre-1920. Published by E. H. Seward, 13 Turton Street, Weymouth. A view along West Street, showing the typical stone terrace of cottages with delightfully random fenestration and the undulating thatch rooves.

Untitled. Written and probably sent in an envelope, headed West Street June 22nd 1912. No publisher. A classic view of the grocer's shop in West Street in the Edwardian era, complete with biscuit tins and enamel advertising signs, and a carefully posed group outside. Standing in the shop doorway is Tommy Toms, one of Abbotsbury's two bakers. The man in the foreground is carrying a basket, perhaps locally made.

Abbotsbury. Postmark 15th November 1904. Published by Walter Cox, Weymouth. A view along West Street towards Market Street and the school, with the grocer's shop in the foreground. Carefully posed on the raised pavement are groups of figures. Standing by the shop are the four Toms brothers, while the woman in the distance is Polly Arnold. The message, to PC Love of the Dorset Constabulary, is to the point and unsigned: "will write tomorrow."

Abbotsbury. Unused, 1920s. Published by Seward, Weymouth. A view along West Street towards the school, showing the cottages on the southern side. Steps were whitewashed to make them visible in the dark.

Abbotsbury. Unused, pre-1914. Published by Weeks & Gimblett, Weymouth. A view westwards along West Street, with Clem Ford's horse and van delivering groceries in an otherwise deserted setting on a bright afternoon. In those days, the village had street lights.

At Abbotsbury. Unused, 1920s. Published by E. A. Sweetman & Son. Another view along West Street, looking westwards, taken near the Market Square.

Untitled. Written but not posted, pre-1914. No publisher. This house in West Street is much later and larger than the typical thatched terraces. The message, a birthday greeting, makes it clear than the house was then called Cotoneasters.

Untitled. Unused, pre-1914. Published by Walter Cox, Weymouth. This view shows Red Lane from the eastern end of West Street. It must have taken the photographer ages to persuade the women and children to take part, pose them, and then make them stand still during the long exposure. Even the cat is cooperating

Abbotsbury. Unused, 1920s. Published by Seward, Weymouth. Rival tearooms, side by side, in Rodden Row, reflect the expansion of tourism in Abbotsbury early in the twentieth century. The nearer one was formerly the old school.

Untitled. Postmark 16th July 1913. Published by R. D. Barratt, Bridport. This card of Rodden Row shows on the right the old Swan public house in West Street. The photograph is much earlier as the pub, and all its terrace, burned down in about 1895.

(Phone) Abbotsbury. 49. Postmark 15th June 1939, posted from Southend-on-Sea to the Bank of England. The Swan Inn was rebuilt on a new site on the Weymouth road beyond Rodden Row. This view shows Bill Hughes, landlord at the time the card was made, presumably to advertise the inn.

Red Lane, Abbotsbury. Unused, 1930s. Published by M. T. Ferry, Abbotsbury. This is the view looking up Red Lane from West Street, with the house called Cotoneasters on the left corner. The telegraph pole helps to date the card.

Red Lane, Abbotsbury. Unused, 1920s. Published by Seward, Weymouth. Another view of Red Lane, this time from the north down towards West Street.

The Grove, Abbotsbury. Unused, pre-1914. Published by R. H. Green, Bristol. A fine view of the pair of cottages in the Grove, now Grove Lane, enlivened by the carefully arranged group of two women and a girl.

The Grove, Abbotsbury. Unused, pre-1914. Published by R. H. Green, Bristol. When this was taken the pair of houses on the left were used as gamekeeper's cottages

Untitled. Unused, dated in pencil 1932. No publisher. Samuel Arnold stands in his garden looking out on to Market Street, photographed at the time he was Chairman of Abbotsbury Parish Council.

Untitled. Unused, pre-1914. No publisher. The old Post Office on the corner of Market Street. The window is filled with brushes, tools and domestic goods, and a poster on the left, headed E. R. (Edward VII) appeals for volunteers for the army. This may date it to the time of the South African war. The postmaster, J.F.Gibbons, is in the doorway.

Abbotsbury. Unused, pre-1914. No publisher. The group of Victorian houses in Market Square, standing out, then as now. The house nearest the school is the old police house.

Market Street, Abbotsbury. Unused, dated in pencil 1929. Published by Seward, Weymouth. This view, probably taken from the church tower, looks along Market Street to the north, with the school at the top in Market Square. A solitary horse and cart makes its way up the otherwise deserted street on a sunny afternoon, probably in early Spring. No doubt a bit later the chimneys will all be smoking.

Abbotsbury. Postmark 2nd October 1944. Published by C. & S. Kestin, Weymouth. Despite the postmark, this is a pre-war view looking up Market Street towards the school, with the Ilchester Arms on the left, marked by the large flag. As in so many Abbotsbury cards, not much is going on. The message says: 'I am still very happy here.'

Market Street, Abbotsbury. Unused, 1960s. Published by A. W. Bourne, Leicester. The Ilchester Arms, with a view down Market Street towards the church, enlivened by a scattering of typical cars of the period. The Ilchester Arms still boasts its grand flag pole, but the flag is in a muddle.

ILCHESTER HOTEL,
ABBOTSBURY, DORSET.

Sea View.

Tea Room.

Ilchester Hotel. Unused advertising postcard, pre-1918. Published by the hotel. Long established and well placed in the centre of Abbotsbury, the Ilchester Arms has been a focal point for the village since the nineteenth century. Early advertisements stress the good sea views, the spacious public rooms, quiet home comforts, personal attention and the billiard room. Much was made of the visit on 15 June 1883 by the Duke and Duchess of Edinburgh and the Duke of Connaught. In 1895 the hotel's owner, T. Cooper, wrote and published The Abbotsbury Guide, a small bound volume which he hoped: 'Performed the task which suggested itself to him, through the many applications from visitors, for the History of Abbotsbury.'

Abbotsbury. Unused, pre-1914. No publisher. The formal facade of the Ilchester Arms commands the Market Place.

Untitled. Unused, pre-1914. Published by J. R. Green, Evershot. A splendid group assembled outside the hotel, ready to depart for a day's outing complete with parasols and post horn.

Abbotsbury. Unused, pre-1914. Published by Hills & Rowney. This view looks down Rodden Row from its eastern end, the section popularly known as Station Road. Apart from the mother and child lurking on the far left, the scene is, as usual, devoid of human life. The character of the village at this time is captured by the unsurfaced road, the creeper-clad stone walls and the overriding sense of peace and quiet.

Corner of Station Road, Abbotsbury. Postmark 1906. Published by J. R. Green, Evershot. This is another example of a potentially ordinary scene, at the far eastern end of the village, made remarkable by the carefully contrived grouping of the figures, an enjoyable feature of so much of the photography of this era. It must have taken ages for the photographer to place his figures in positions that suggested casual informality but were actually quite the opposite.

55

The Station, Abbotsbury. Unused, pre-1914. Published by Seward, Weymouth. Authorised in 1877 and opened on 8th November 1885, the six-mile Abbotsbury Railway was inspired partly by tourism and partly by hoped-for traffic from iron ore deposits in the hills behind the village. In the event, neither materialised, although in its early days the railway was quite busy, as this card suggests.

Untitled. Unused, pre-1918. published by R. H. Green, Bristol. With its handsome stone station with tall chimneys and broad canopies, the Abbotsbury Railway had an individuality that survived its absorption into the GWR network in 1896. Passengers and staff pose for the photographer, while the GWR push-pull auto-train waits in the background.

Untitled. Unused, pre-1918. Published by E. H. Seward, Weymouth. Despite its failure to fulfill the hopes of its promoters, the Abbotsbury branch played its part in the life of the village. The train brought supplies and visitors to Abbotsbury, and took away local produce. While the engine driver watches the photographer, others busy themselves loading and unloading the guard's compartment. Soap and a milk churn stand on the platform, along with some large wicker hampers. There are also two prams, one with baby, but no sign of the mothers.

Untitled. Unused, 1920s. No publisher. Increasingly little used, the branch was closed in 1952. This view, looking towards the end of the line, shows the famous station gardens, and the long platform, built in hope of bigger trains and better things.

Untitled. Unused, 1920s. No publisher. In its heyday, the railway brought large numbers of people to Abbotsbury. This busy scene depicts a Sunday School outing, complete with dogs, prams and children of all ages, preparing to have their picnic in the fields above the station. The train brought them, and in due course will return them safely to Weymouth.

Untitled. Unused, 1920s. No publisher. From an early date the railway suffered from road competition. Here, a charabanc prepares to set off from Weymouth on "A Pretty Drive to Abbotsbury" taking in all the sights. The passengers seem to be looking forward to the trip, even though the boy in the driving seat is much too young for the job.

58

Untitled. Unused, 1920s. No publisher. The Strangways family have been associated with Abbotsbury since the early sixteenth century. In the eighteenth century Elizabeth Strangways Horner married Stephen Fox, who became the first Earl of Ilchester. This card shows Lord Stavordale, the eldest son, with a saddle presented to him by the people of Abbotsbury to celebrate his coming of age.

Lady Ilchester, Lady Powis, Lady Guiness, Sir Donald Wallace, HRH of Wales, Lady Crewe. Unused. Published by J. R. Green, Evershot. A group assembled with the Princess of Wales on 8 December 1904.

HRH Princess of Wales and Lady Stavordale. Abbotsbury. 8 Dec 1904. Unused. Published by J. R. Green, Evershot.

HRH Prince of Wales, Abbotsbury, 8 Dec 1904. Unused. No publisher. A great event in the history of Abbotsbury was the Royal Visit of December 1904, and many cards commemorate it. The Royal couple came to join a shooting party organised by the Earl of Ilchester, and members of aristocratic families, dignitaries and local worthies took part. This and the card below show the Prince of Wales, later George V, and other participants prior to the shoot.

Untitled. Unused. No publisher. The Prince of Wales is third from the left.

Untitled. Unused. No publisher. Photographed soon after their wedding on 24 May 1924, Lady Mary Fox Strangways and her husband, Captain Herbert pose with the presents given them by the village.

Untitled. Unused, pre-1914. No publisher. Old Spanish ships' cannons, raised from Lyme Bay, were put on display on the hillside below the castle. This group are admiring their handiwork, having reset the cannons on to new, rough-hewn log supports.

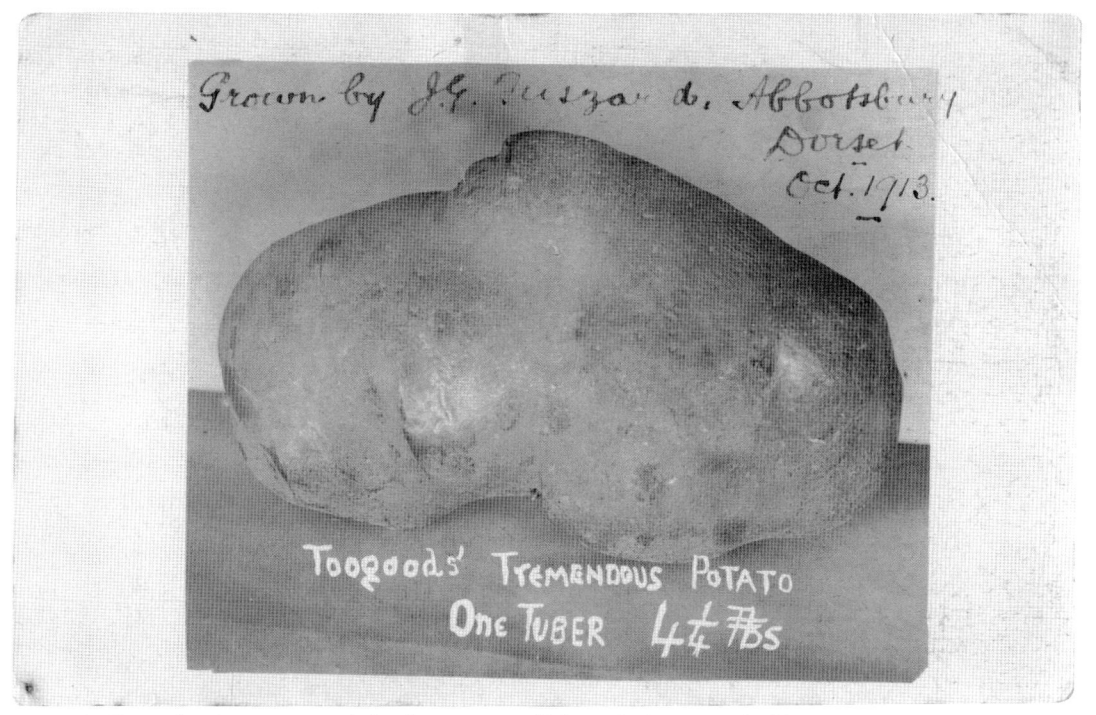

Toogood's Tremendous Potato. Unused, dated 1913. No publisher. This bizarre card celebrates a massive potato grown in Abbotsbury in 1913 and displayed by J. G. Fuzzard.

Untitled. Unused, 1920s. No publisher. A group of potato pickers, left to right E. Bartlett, R. Bridle, George Limm, unknown, Punch Hayne. Sadly, no J. G. Fuzzard, the master potato grower.

Untitled. Unused, 1920s. No publisher. Rare visitors to Abbotsbury, pausing on their way to a circus at Weymouth. The elephant and the pony look relaxed enough, but the dog in the lady's arms is not so sure.

Untitled. Unused, pre-1918. No publisher. Photographed in Back Street, Albert Stokes takes a break from his delivery round for W. C. Hodder, Abbotsbury's butcher. Cart, horse and traces are all well turned out.

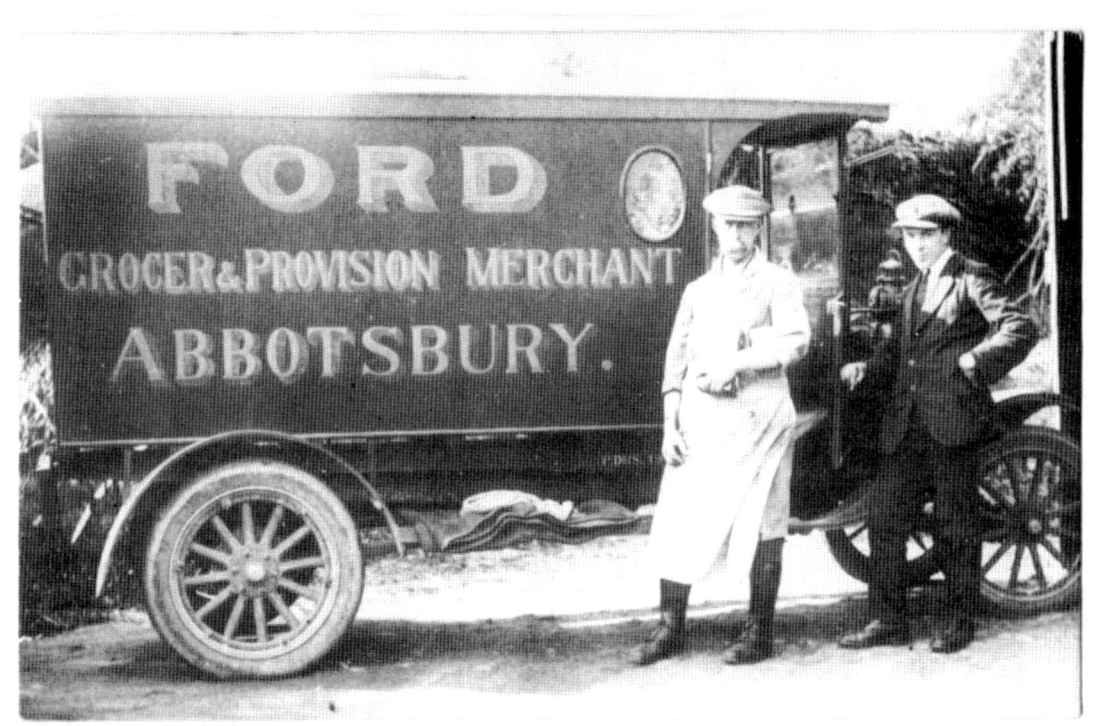

Untitled. Unused, 1920s. No publisher. Ford's delivery van, with Clem Ford and Bill Ferry posing in front of it. The Fords were a long-established village family and farmers at Clayhanger. They also ran both grocery shops in Market Street, one of which became a teashop.

Untitled. Unused, 1920s. Published by Jerome. Bill Ferry outside Ford's shop in Market Street. The window displays are filled with familiar names: Typhoo, Fry, Ridgway, Bovril, Oxo, Woodbine, Mansion House, Kensitas, Puritan Soap.

Abbotsbury. Postmark 1947. No publisher. Members of the I.B.R.A group in the Congregational Chapel in Back Street, celebrating either ten or thirty years of their religious organisation, as notices in the background suggest both dates. The organisation was clearly founded in 1881 and so, judging by the costume, the most likely date is 1911. The late postmark date is an added complication, explained partly by the writer's comment: 'As you can see, I was "stuck" for a card again, please take care of it.'

Untitled. Unused, 1920s. No publisher. The Abbotsbury Girl Guide troop, outside the village school.

Untitled. Unused, about 1925. No publisher. The pupils of Abbotsbury school, with their headteacher Mr Rintoull, everyone looking spick and span, and some girls in guide uniform

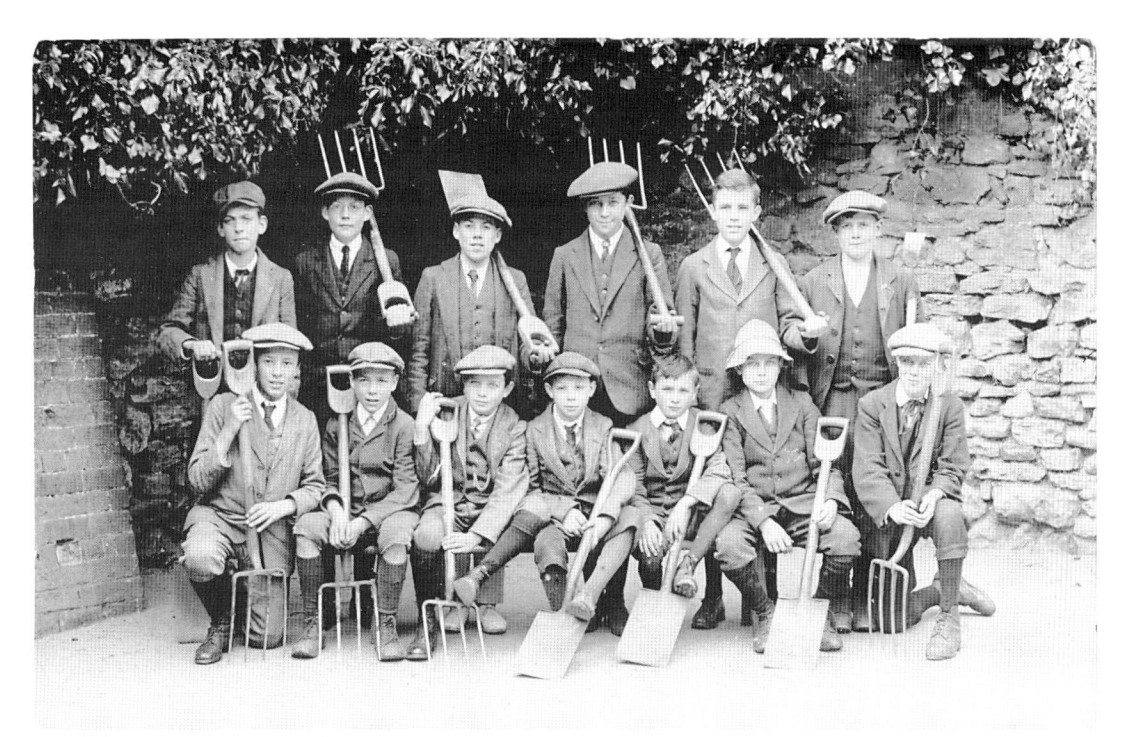

Untitled. Unused, 1920s. No publisher. This delightful card shows the Gardening Class at Abbotsbury school, most wearing their dads' caps.

Untitled. Unused, 1920s. No publisher. Abbotsbury Tennis Club, complete with two dog members, gathered around the fierce-looking Mrs Hawkins.

Untitled. Unused, dated 1931. Photograph by S. J. Herbert, Weymouth. The Abbotsbury Cricket Club, with the Dorset Daily Echo Cup. Back: B. Corbett, C. Hodder, G. Thurol, W. Eley, J. Cutler, G. Kerley. Front: W Alford, C. Hutchings, M. Cribb, J. Hayne, J. Daubeney and W. Burden.

Untitled. Unused. No publisher. The new coastguard cottages were built in 1926. Grouped together here in front of the newly completed buildings are those responsible for their planning and construction.

Untitled. Unused, 1940s. No publisher. Photographed formally against the background of the barn, this is a group of local Observer Corps volunteers, in about 1940. Included are members of the Cribb, Burt, Limm, Hutchings, Dunford, Toms, Hayns, Forder, Vivian, Arnold and Lexster families.

TRFA Dorset. Abbotsbury Camp July 1908. Unused. Published by Hare, Bridport. Territorial and other volunteer regiments held their annual camps in many parts of west Dorset. This shows the Royal Field Artillery's camp at Abbotsbury.

TRFA Dorset. Abbotsbury Camp July 1908. Unused. Published by Hare, Bridport.

Untitled. Unused, about 1940. No publisher. The Abbotsbury Home Guard. Back: A. Huddy, T. Price, W. Limm, L. Toms, M. Ford, S. Spicer, G. Horlock, A. Hayne. Centre: J. Churchill, E. Bartlett, G. Gill, W. Arnold, W. Roper, G. Ford, T. Horlock. Front: W. Ford, R. Joyce, C. Hutchings, S. Price, A. Lewington, G. Gill, W. Dunford.

Untitled. Unused, about 1940. No publisher. D. Hutchings and W. Dunford carrying out Observer Corps duty at Chapel Tower on St Catherine's Hill

Hospital Fete July 20th 1908. Unused. No publisher. Villagers dressed as Dorset rustics, with echoes of Hardy. Second left, Tess ? is Charles Ford.

Untitled. Unused, 1930s. Published by S. J. Herbert, Weymouth. This card shows the annual Garland Day ceremony, held in May, when traditionally the children of each fishing family would parade with garlands to be taken out to sea and thrown in as offerings, to ensure a good season. The flags and bunting suggest this may be 1935, the Jubilee year.

Untitled. Unused. No publisher. The Silver Jubilee of 1935 was an excuse for nation-wide celebration. In Abbotsbury, among other events, there was a parade of decorated vehicles. Here, Godfrey White's car leads the procession along Rodden Row, followed by Cyril Daubeny. His wife, dressed as Gerty the Gangster, is standing in the sunroof.

Untitled. Unused, 1935. No publisher. Arthur Hutchings took the theme Beer is Best, and won second prize.

Untitled. Unused, 1935, published by S. J. Herbert, Weymouth. Bill Hughes, the landlord of the old Swan, won first prize in the Trade Section of the Jubilee Parade. His lorry carried the Abbotsbury band.

Untitled. Unused, 1935. Published by Jerome Ltd. In the Jubilee parade John Wood's vehicle, hidden beneath masses of greenery, made the most of the garden theme.

Untitled. Unused, 1935. No publisher. The Cribb family prepare for the decorated motorcycle section of the Jubilee Parade. Young Gordon watches, his grandfather stands in the doorway, while his father Monty prepares to drive away, with Gordon's grandmother on the pillion, looking rather serious.

Untitled. Unused, 1935. Published by S. J. Herbert, Weymouth. Charlie and Olive Trevett ready for the Jubilee Parade, with Jim Trevett and Mrs Pitcher in the wonderfully decorated sidecar.

Coronation Parade, Abbotsbury. Unused, 1937. Published by Seward, Weymouth. The coronation of George VI and Queen Mary was another excuse for national celebration, and for another parade of decorated vehicles in Abbotsbury. A surprisingly small number of spectators watch the parade get under way.

Coronation Parade, Abbotsbury. Unused, 1937. Published by Seward, Weymouth.

Untitled. Unused, 1937. Published by S. J. Herbert, Weymouth. A fancy dress group ready for the Coronation Parade: the Roper family, blacked up, Clara Keech, Walt Dunford and the Gill family.

Untitled. Unused, 1937. Published by S. J. Herbert, Weymouth. Another entrant for the Coronation Parade, the Dunford family's Gipsy Ragtime Band. Will Eley, dressed as a sweep, holds the horse

Digging & Tunnelling for "Badger" at Abbotsbury, Dorset. Unused, pre-1918. No publisher. Though frowned upon today, such scenes were a normal part of village life. The dog, raring to go, is being held back for the photograph. Note the large jar of cider.

Untitled. Unused, pre-1918. No publisher. Mr Wren, the gamekeeper, with staff and dogs, surrounding a captured badger, successfully dug out of its tunnel.

The Cattistock Hunt at Abbotsbury. Unused, pre-1914. Published by Seward, Weymouth. The Meet in the Square at Abbotsbury was always a popular part of the Cattistock's calendar, even though there were many other meeting places near the village, including Askerswell, Upwey and Portesham. The hunt gathers on a bright winter's day, ready for the off, while the school children line up to watch from behind the school railings.

The Cattistock Hounds, Abbotsbury. Unused, 1920s. Published by Seward, Weymouth

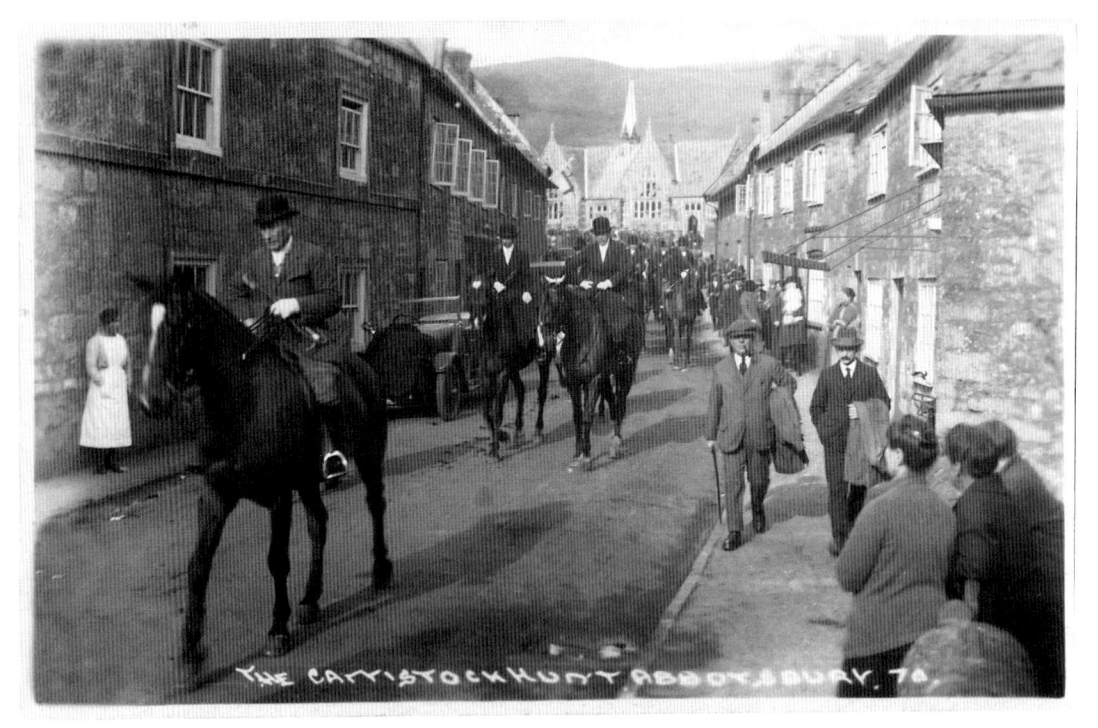

The Cattistock Hunt, Abbotsbury. Unused, 1920s. Published by Seward, Weymouth. Followed by a massive crowd of supporters, the Hunt sets off down Market Street.

The Cattistock Hunt at Abbotsbury. Unused, pre-1918. Published by Seward, Weymouth. The hunt sets off along West Street on a winter Saturday, accompanied by a gaggle of local children, all well-dressed and out of school.

Mackerel Fishing at Abbotsbury. Unused, pre-1914. No publisher. Fishing from Chesil was still a major local enterprise when this card was issued. Shown here is Bill Ferry, far right, the owner of one of the boats, with his crew, displaying their catch of mackerel. At this time, there were about ten boats active in Abbotsbury, and in a good season of ample catches, fish would be auctioned straight off the boats to wholesale buyers from Bath, Bristol, Southampton and London. The fish were transported by train. Traditionally, the takings were shared out by the captain on Saturday evening, accompanied by beer and bread and cheese, the helpings of which reflected the success, or otherwise, of the week's fishing.

Untitled. Unused, dated 1924. No publisher. A typical Abbotsbury fishing crew, left to right, Sam Pittman, Tommy Pitcher, Harold Dunford, Albert Roper, Fred Roper, Jimmy Lake, Johnny Limm (in front with fish), Arthur Gill, Punch Hayne, Gabriel Mundy, Harry Dart, Jim Bryer.

Fishing at Abbotsbury. Clearing the Nets. Unused, pre-1918. Published by R. H. Green, Bristol. Bill Ferry, in bowler hat, with his crew, unloading a haul of mackerel. Traditionally, fishing never took place on Sunday, and Ferry, a religious man, maintained this ancient custom.

Untitled. Unused, 1950s. No publisher. These two cards show the technique of seine net fishing, the most common form used by Abbotsbury fishing crews. A boat takes the net out to sea, dragging it into a curve so it forms a giant bag. The team on shore then haul the net into the beach, gradually reducing the size of the bag until all the fish are together, as shown below. the net is then opened out on the beach, and the fish loaded into baskets.

Untitled. Unused, 1920s. No publisher. These cards show Ash Huddy's crew at work, the last full time seine net fishermen at Abbotsbury. The technique has now died out.

Abbotsbury Beach. Unused, pre-1918. Published by R. H. Green, Bristol. Despite its often bleak and windy appearance, the stretch of Chesil Bank adjacent to Abbotsbury was a popular beach, as seen here in the Edwardian era. Typically, everyone is rather well dressed.

On the Beach, Abbotsbury. Unused, 1930s. Published by Tuck & Sons. On a warm day, the beach has attracted a number of visitors who are making the most of Chesil's rather exposed pebble beach.

Ashore at Abbotsbury. Feb 14th 1914. Unused. Published by J. R. Potts, Bridport. Many ships have come to grief on Chesil Bank over the centuries. This card shows the Dutch steamer Dorothea, 3,500 tons, loaded with iron ore, driven ashore in a gale on to the beach in a storm in 1914.

Wreck on the Chesil Beach at Abbotsbury. Unused, 1914. Published by Seward, Weymouth. The Dorothea firmly on the beach, with the salvage tug Lyons in attendance. After unloading her cargo, she was refloated in November the same year.

Untitled. Unused, 1914. No publisher. The Dorothea, under the command of Captain Wagner, had a crew of 22. The captain and the chief engineer spent some time in Abbotsbury, waiting for the ship to be refloated. This photograph shows the two Dutchmen with the Daubeney family.

The Coastguards Station Abbotsbury Dorset. Unused, about 1930. Published by Seward, Weymouth. The new coastguard cottages and lookout station were completed in 1926 and remained in use until there were no more full time coastguards in Abbotsbury. the coastguards are in residence as the flag is flying.

Abbotsbury Gardens. Monkey Puzzle. Unused, pre-1914. Published by R. H. Green, Bristol. The origins of the semi-tropical gardens at Abbotsbury go back to the time of Elizabeth, 1st Countess of Ilchester and today certain plants, notably the camellias, can be traced back to the eighteenth century. Developed over several generations, the gardens have always been popular with visitors since the Victorian period. A number of early postcards show various features of the garden and its unusual trees and plants.

Pampas Grass, Abbotsbury. Unused, 1930s. Published by Kestins, Weymouth. Pampas grasses and specimen trees line the approach road to the gardens.

Abbotsbury Gardens. Cabbage Palm. Unused, pre-1914. Published by J. R. Green, Evershot. Exotic plants and carefully posed children, a popular combination in the Edwardian era.

Abbotsbury Gardens. Rustic Bridge. Postmark 31st May 1909. Published by J. R. Green, Evershot. There were many sections of the garden, featuring exotic plants from all over the world, including Japan. An 1899 catalogue lists over 5000 species. This card, sent to Newton Abbot, says: 'Have just been to Abbotsbury & return to Weymouth. Had a glorious day.'

Abbotsbury Gardens. Water Lily Ponds. Unused, pre-1914. Published by R. H. Green, Bristol.

Untitled. Unused, dated 1938, and sent as a Christmas card. Published by Jerome. Joe Gill and Fred Lexster, Swanherd, outside the decoy man's cottage at the Swannery.

Abbotsbury Swannery. Unused, pre-1914. Published by R. H. Green, Bristol. Swans have probably been at Abbotsbury at least since the eleventh century, when the monastery was established. Equally ancient is the role of Swanherd, the person responsible for the herd. This shows Gregory Gill, who held the office from the 1890s.

Abbotsbury Swannery. Unused, 1920s. No publisher. The Swanherd surveys his charges on a quiet day by the Fleet.

Untitled. Unused, Possibly 1930s. No publisher. The Swanherd Charles Roper, with some of his charges.

The Swannery, Abbotsbury. Unused, 1930s. Published in the West Dorset series. The most famous of recent Swanherds was Fred Lexster, who died in 1982. He was well known for his radio and television broadcasts.

Swan with Cygnets. Unused, 1920s. Published by Seward, Weymouth. Legally, all swans belong to the Queen. The only exceptions are those on the Thames, which belong to the Company of Vintners and Dyers, and the Abbotsbury herd, owned initially by the monastery, and subsequently by the Strangways family.

Untitled. Postmark 19th August 1905. No publisher. This appears to have been sent by the photographer, W. J. Masters, as the message says: 'What do you think of my photo. I have 13 different pictures of these.'

Abbotsbury Swannery. Unused, pre-1918. Published by R. H. Green, Bristol. There are over 130 pairs of swans at Abbotsbury, raising a similar number of cygnets each year. As wild birds, the swans come and go at will. The herd is only managed during nesting time, and during the raising of cygnets.,

Abbotsbury Swannery. Nesting Time. Unused, pre-1914. Published by R. H. Green, Bristol. This card shows the Swanherd, Gregory Gill, surveying his swans at nesting time.

Abbotsbury Swannery. Unused, 1920s. No publisher. Established in 1655, the duck decoy is one of only five still in use in Britain Used originally to catch ducks for food, the decoy is now a means of ringing and recording all birds that enter the two 'pipes' one of which is shown here.

The Smugglers Cave, Abbotsbury. Unused, pre-1918. Published by R. H. Green, Bristol. Many stories were associated with the cave on Folly Hill, with its interior compartments. The caves are probably a legacy from iron ore excavations in the nineteenth century.

Untitled. Unused, 1920s. No publisher. Despite its mild climate, Abbotsbury has known some severe winters, with deep snow blocking the roads and lanes of the village. Now, snow is quite a rarity, and never lasts long. The winters of 1962-3 and 1986 were the most severe in recent memory.